HOW TO RUN A MARATHON

Dressed in sweat-soaked running kit, complete with a
head and a wrist band, a black plastic bin-liner, or
designer jogging shorts, the marathon runner emerges
from the growing dusk to terrify small children and dogs.
Runners have their own private language; their own
strange apparel; their peculiar customs. Most, if not all,
are masochists of a special kind.

HOW TO RUN A MARATHON is essential reading for
marathon runners, their partners and spectators.
Runners cannot be stopped by floods, Arctic conditions,
nuclear strikes or the heat death of the universe; they
survive against all odds, to stagger on to the finishing
line. Here we are introduced to The Pantomime Horse,
The Incredible Bulk, The Shuffler, The Apparition, The
Iron Man and many others. If you can't break the pain
barrier or do your personal best, then you can at least
join Tony Benyon and Kevin Macey in some
après-marathon refreshment.

About the Authors

Anthony Benyon attended the Hornsey College of Art where he studied industrial design. Before becoming a full time cartoonist he lectured at the Sir John Cass College of Art. He became a cartoonist for *NME* which has printed the cartoon strip *The Lone Groover* for many years. *The Lone Groover* has also seen life as a record, magazine, book, T shirt, radio sketches and badge. He has worked in most areas of the music business. Anthony Benyon is now a copywriter and art director in advertising.

Kevin Macey was born in North London and educated at Highgate School and St Martin's School of Art. He has been a freelance cartoonist since 1974. He has worked for *Foul* magazine, the alternative football paper, *Time Out* and *The Times*. The publications to which he currently contributes include *The Health and Social Services Journal* and *The Times Literary Supplement*. He frequently does work for sports advertising. His advertising work also includes Fosters Lager, Nestles and Elastoplast.

Both authors live in London.

HOW TO RUN A
MARATHON

Tony Benyon and Kevin Macey

NEW ENGLISH LIBRARY
Hodder and Stoughton

Copyright © 1986 by Tony Benyon and
Kevin Macey/Bookbourne Limited

First published in Great Britain in 1986 by
New English Library
New English Library Paperback Edition 1987

British Library C.I.P.

Benyon, Tony
How to run a marathon.
1. Marathon running—Anecdotes, facetiae,
satire, etc.
I. Title   II. Macey, Kevin
796.4'26   GV1065

ISBN 0-450-40911-2

Printed and bound in Great Britain for
Hodder and Stoughton Paperbacks, a
division of Hodder and Stoughton Ltd.,
Mill Road, Dunton Green, Sevenoaks,
Kent (Editorial Office: 47 Bedford
Square, London WC1B 3DP) by
St Edmundsbury Press Ltd.,
Bury St Edmunds, Suffolk.

CONTENTS

INTRODUCTION

On the surface it would appear that running is one of the most natural things a human being can do and, like breathing, it is possible to do it for free. Nothing could be further from the truth. A price must be paid.

An acquaintance of mine entered the second London Marathon and trained for it for fifty weeks. Three quarters of the way through this period he was running in his local park deep in thought. His wife had finally left him the previous evening convinced he was having clandestine meetings with a lover while out training. Their deteriorating relationship had caused him to lose concentration at work and a junior colleague to be promoted over him.

This already sad man was suddenly dragged to the ground by three Alsatians. His life was saved only by the intervention of the owner. Staggering to his feet, his nerve snapped and he cursed the owner with every foul oath known to man, and after threatening to give him a good kicking he walked away promising to call the police.

Apologetically, the stranger informed him that he was a policeman. In fact, he was a police dog handler and the foaming creatures were also a bona fide part of the constabulary. Feeling crushed by fate, he returned home with only his obsessive thoughts of the marathon to give him strength. Alas, two weeks before the race, a cyclist ran into him and broke his ankle. In his own philosophical words, 'there is always a price to pay for having a good time'.

Introduction

Many of you reading this book will be beginners to marathon running and may not be at all used to physical exercise. It would be dangerous for you to proceed any further without first checking whether your physical condition will allow you to read the following pages. Simply read the questions below.

1. Are you an obese mound of quivering, wheezing jelly?
2. Do you have chest pains, feel dizzy and keep falling over?
3. Are you a big mouth who accepted a drunken wager to run The Marathon?
4. Do you have suicidal tendencies?
5. Do you have the requisite number of legs (2)?
6. Do you have a cigarette before you wake up in the morning?
7. Are you in labour?
8. Do you think Wombats should have the vote?

If you answer any of these questions in the affirmative you need medical attention. If you answered them all in the affirmative then prepare yourself for longterm medical and psychiatric treatment.

8

CHAPTER 1

WHAT
TO WEAR

RUNNING KIT

The clothes people choose to wear while running are just as diverse and bizarre as the reasons why they wish to run in the first place. It is not uncommon during a marathon to be passed by a pantomime horse or a blindfolded chef running backwards while preparing a three-course meal. Charity runners and other deranged extroverts who want to live out their unnatural fantasies in public have carte blanche when it comes to dress. Alas, the orthodox or serious runners are restricted to a more conventional appearance. They have to look the very epitome of serious runners until the day comes when their sponsors want them to dress as chocolate bars or tins of food to earn their substantial fees. Earning a 'Fast buck' will soon lead to equally 'Fast food'. Meanwhile the first-time runner must select clothes that he or she feels comfortable wearing. Charity runners should visit a fancy dress shop and book the costumes they find the most appealing, while the poseurs who have yet to jog one foot in front of the other should get out their credit cards and prepare to spend.

SHOES

On entering a modern sports shop you will be amazed by the rows and rows of designer running shoes. Do not make the mistake of falling in love with the ones that match your eyes or the ones that make your heart beat faster because of some inexplicable chemical reaction between you.

Shoes that look wonderful but don't fit can be dangerous because they cause sores and blisters. And if they are too big and you have a high running action one could fly off and knock out a pedestrian's eye. Even worse, your shoe could fly through the open window of a passing truck and stun the driver causing him to crash into a supermarket killing hundreds of shoppers. Would you want this on your conscience?

The types of shoes on sale are incredibly varied; there are shoes fitted with stabilizers, computers, digital grips, graphic equalizers and countless other electronic gadgets. In the future when you put on your running shoes they will automatically sink hypodermic needles into your feet to place you in suspended animation while the shoes complete the race for you.

It is important to remember to buy your shoes in the afternoon because this is the time of day when your feet are at their largest. I'm not sure of the right time of day to buy a jogging bra, but similarly you should try on both shoes because one foot is also larger than the other.

Shoes

SOCKS

Runners sometimes elect to run in shoes without socks, but less frequently run in socks without shoes. The purpose of the sock is to offer the foot protection from those parts of the shoe that rub against it. But it is essential to keep your socks clean because if they get stiffened with dried sweat they can cause as much damage to your feet as shoes and also screw up your social life.

If you wear double-soled cotton or woollen socks but find you have to stop every two miles to squeeze out the excess moisture, then you should change to a synthetic material that dries out faster.

Sadly, socks have been known to break up marriages, and anyone cursed by particularly moist or pungent feet should remember to put their socks out at night, preferably in a sealed plastic bag. If you toss them out of the back door without sealing them up you will wake in the morning to find several stunned cats on your door step.

However, their pungency can work to your benefit. Horticulturists claim that some socks buried in a flower bed act as a superb deterrent to slugs.

The fashion of the moment is the short sock, but it is believed manufacturers will soon be bringing out the long sock which will offer the professional runner more room for carrying advertising.

Socks

SHORTS

Baggy knee-length shorts are a thing of the past. Today's thing is maximum leg exposure, shorts with thigh-high splits at the sides or even more recently, shorts that look increasingly like swimming trunks. Doubtless runners will soon appear on the streets in jock straps and G-strings; they will be luminous, of course, to help night drivers.

The ideal pair of shorts must not be tight around the waist but secure enough not to drop to the ground after the wearer has taken half a dozen strides. A runner without confidence in his or her shorts can suffer a spiralling anxiety effect which can increase the pulse rate alarmingly.

The material shorts are made of cannot be too light in weight. Hand-knitted shorts absorb moisture and will drop to the ground during heavy rain. Synthetic materials are lighter, less abrasive and dry more quickly. They also come in the most delightful colours which makes accessorising more fun and provides you with a better chance of matching your eyes.

Men mainly wear swimming trunks or a jock strap under their shorts while women prefer cotton briefs. As yet the boom in split crotch lace sporting panties has not materialised; which doesn't mean to say it won't.

Shorts

VESTS

Wearing a string vest during the summer months will give you the appearance of a seasoned runner. Even more modern is the vest with the mesh midriff and the satin strip across the chest. Not only is it the poseur's delight but it also stops jogger's nipple while still allowing the navel to breathe.

Try to avoid wearing 'Sub Four Minute' vests while you are still at the staggering stage; even stray dogs will spot you as a fake. It is also advisable not to wear vests with such slogans as 'Marathon runners do it for hours on end' otherwise you will become instantly unpopular with the serious runners whom you may want to impress.

However, in these days of sponsorship it is quite acceptable to wear vests that carry some form of advertising extolling the virtues of a local garage or restaurant, but avoid any products that may encourage people to stop you in the street while you are running and ask you for brochures. Having your training runs interrupted is not beneficial.

Greengrocers' advertising should never be accepted. It can be a great embarrassment to a woman if she has to run through the streets with 'Ripe Melons' written across her chest or for a man to have 'Fresh Fruit' emblazoned across his; a training run can easily turn into a pursuit.

TRACK SUITS

The track suit is ideal wear for the shy runner. Dressing in one is like putting on camouflage; the wearer is instantly lost against a backdrop of thousands of other track-suited people going about their everyday lives.

Track suits are worn for almost every activity, be it playing tennis, football or reggae. Soon, young executives working in the City will be jogging to their offices wearing pin-striped track suits and perhaps even Her Majesty, the Queen, may one day be seen running through Westminster in a pink, bejewelled track suit on her way to open Parliament.

For most people wearing a track suit is more than a way of saying 'Look at me! I'm not restricted by tight trousers; that's why my sex life is so good!' It is also a way of saying 'Hey! I've got the kind of freedom in my life that you're missing out on, and I'm also thinking of becoming a vegetarian.'

When buying a track suit, make sure the colour matches your complexion and the trousers are not flared otherwise you will not only look like a Las Vegas crooner but you will also get blasts of icy air up your legs on cold mornings. It is also necessary for the trousers not to be too wide otherwise they will act as sails in a gale and sap your energy when you're running into a headwind.

Hoods are considered unhip; they are worn only by boxers and bank robbers.

Track Suits

CHAPTER 2

HOW TO TRAIN

WALKING AND STANDING

In simple terms a competitor completes a marathon by remaining upright while moving forwards until the finishing line has been crossed.

Most people with sedentary jobs don't stand up for more than twenty minutes at any time during the day. So a beginner should become used to standing for more than four hours a day before he can even consider running. If you are the sort of person who watches television from eight in the evening to midnight try to watch it standing up. You will have to start gently by standing during the television commercials and take a rest during the programmes. When you gain in confidence move on to standing up during the news or cartoon shorts gradually building up to programmes the length of Dallas or Dynasty. (It may be hard to do without falling asleep so scatter cushions onto the floor around you). Avoid alcohol because it can also cause muscle relaxation leading to complete leglessness.

When you have become proficient at standing, the next step is to learn how to move forwards; the easiest form of this is walking. Practise walking in shopping areas where there are the sorts of crowds that you are likely to meet at the start of a race trampling all over your feet and elbowing you in the tenderest of places.

Walking and Standing

RUNNING

Many first-time runners find the psychological aspects of starting to run the most difficult. For example, if one leaves through the front door wearing a running kit will the neighbours fall from their windows in fits of laughter or will the local children aim hurtful and wounding comments at you? A fear of being vulnerable to a sarcastic and vicious world is quite common.

To counteract this feeling of inadequacy, it is essential to adopt one of two techniques. Firstly, there is the nocturnal training technique practised when prying eyes are at a minimum. Secondly, there is the 'I'm not really running at all technique' which involves wearing everyday clothes, carrying a briefcase or handbag, walking through the front door quite normally and then starting to trot as though running for a train, all the time consulting your wrist watch to emphasise your lateness. By doing this you give the appearance of being a pedestrian in a hurry and not a pedestrian runner on a maiden run.

Of course, there are some who don't mind bounding into the street in expensive runing clothes and collapsing after five yards. They are known as exhibitionists and if they didn't do outrageous things now and again their neighbours would be concerned about them.

Training Routes

DOGS

Dogs are one of the greatest dangers to runners. Only one thing is more dangerous than a dog and that is its owner. When you are pinned to the ground by a snarling, rabid beast with stained fangs and bad breath its owner is more likely to kick you than apologise. In his eyes you are either shouting too loudly at his pet (even though you are shouting for mercy) or you are bleeding too freely over his beast's freshly washed and permed coat.

Dog owners are amongst the most thoughtless people in the universe. Not only do they accuse you of blunting their pet's fangs after they have gnawed off one of your limbs but they also encourage their hounds to deposit their droppings along the highway causing a runner to go into an uncontrollable skid if he runs into them at speed.

How can you avoid dogs? Alas, the truth is that you can't. Whenever you hear the name 'Tiny' called out be on your guard, because 'Tiny' is certain to be an Alsatian who has a taste for human blood.

Carrying a baseball bat when you are out running won't help. If you so much as bend the eyelash of the beast salivating after you then your fate would almost assuredly be a public hanging. A drugged steak, preferably well-sharpened, is the most useful defensive ploy.

Dogs

How To Train

CARS

Cars are almost as great a danger to runners as dogs. You may be harmlessly running along a pavement when suddenly the door of a parked car flies open causing you to crash into it. While you are lying on the ground counting stars, the owner of the vehicle will be frothing at the mouth demanding to know the name of your insurance company because the bone sticking out of your shoulder has scratched the paintwork. Drunken drivers are the worst. They have the habit of pursuing you down country lanes and up grass embankments, all the while laughing like maniacs behind the wheel. They are also accurate shots with beer cans which they aim at your head. One of the sights they seem to enjoy most is of runners hurling themselves through plate glass windows in an attempt to escape. Some running experts will tell you it is advisable to wear white or light clothing at night to make yourself easily seen by oncoming drivers. Beware! Light colours only make you a more identifiable target. In addition to running you into the ground, drivers have another method for eliminating runners; it's called carbon monoxide. The deadly gas is pumped directly out of the car's exhaust straight into your lungs. A mask does offer some protection, but running along the street wearing a mask will cause you to be coshed to the ground by the police. Even worse, you may be chased by a police dog handler.

Cars

THE WEATHER

Always try to run with the wind behind you because running into it can be an enormous strain. It also dries out your skin and deprives you of that healthy, soft, fresh look that you so desperately desire.

If circumstances contrive to have you running into a head wind all you can do is to ensure that your clothing is not too baggy. The least wind-resistant way to run is naked. This is known as streaking and is frowned upon by marathon runners everywhere except in California.

When the snow is on the ground, take up skiing; and when ice is about, take up skating or stay indoors. Running in such conditions can be very dangerous in urban areas when it is not possible to stop or take corners correctly.

In the summer, if you suddenly become confused, dizzy and start to vomit while suffering from diarrhoea, the chances are that you are suffering from heat stroke after running out in the sun for too long. Immediate attention from a doctor is necessary. However, when you are in such a condition you will find it impossible to contact a doctor and no one else is going to help you; only your mother would come anywhere near you in that disgusting state. So stay out of the sun.

Rain is soothing for runners unless it turns into flash flooding. Hail stones can be a problem, but only if they are very large or you are very small.

The Weather

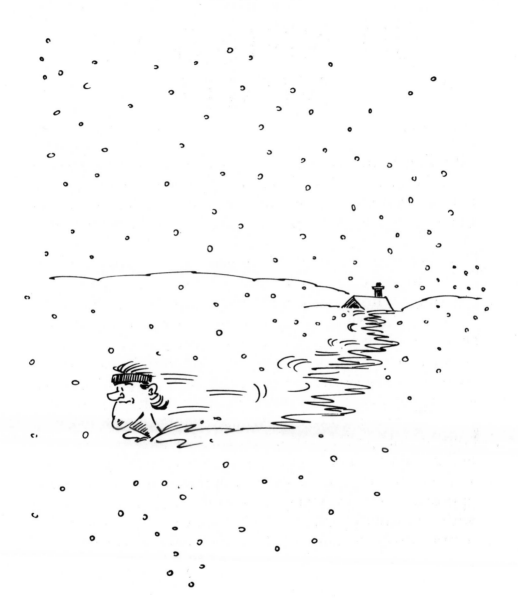

RUNNING AT NIGHT

Running at night is not something a person with a nervous disposition should do. For some of you dark shadows may hold a certain terror, and quite rightly so with mad axemen and drug-crazed multiple murderers with chain saws lying in wait.

However, to some extent the streets of major cities can be safe if you are only lightly armed and fortunately most junk-sodden, gun-happy snipers find it extremely difficult to control their shakes long enough to hit a moving target.

Drivers with their brains addled by cheap drink and income tax forms are a common problem, as are the potholes in roads which can cause you to twist an ankle or even break a leg, leaving you alone and helpless in the dark and easy prey for demented weirdos or scavenging wolves.

Some people prefer to run at dawn. The air is at its cleanest and it can be a breath-taking experience best accompanied by a Walkman playing some appropriately spiritual music as opposed to 'Heavy Metal'. But remember not to sing along with it too loudly or you will give away your position in the empty streets to a nearby dope fiend in search of a victim.

ON SEEING GOD

Many people claim that on certain runs they have achieved a state of perfect bliss or ecstasy, and that on rare occasions they have been warmed by what can best be described as a spiritual or religious experience. Such statements have resulted in other people usually more at home with a joint taking up running. Their main hope is to reach a level of mind-blowing euphoria.

Such is the reason why many weirdos and loonies are attracted to running. It has been suggested by more serious runners that licenses should be provided for runners only after a psychiatric report gives them a clean bill of health. Others believe the damage is done *after* they have taken up running, because of the constant jogging and shaking the brain experiences.

However, there is little doubt a 'high' can be achieved by certain runners in the right circumstances. For example, when the mind and a physically perfect body reach a glorious balance, a sensation of being able to run and run forever hand in hand with God fills the runner's consciousness. Or when a very average runner happens to be running past a glue factory when it is on maximum production and the wind is in the right direction.

On Seeing God

CHAPTER 3

THE EFFECT OF RUNNING

YOUR SEX LIFE

Without a doubt running can alter your sex life drastically. The early days of training reduce you to a mound of aching jelly barely able to crawl unassisted upstairs let alone indulge in any nocturnal naughties. Quite naturally, this can cause distress in the marriage partner, speeding up an impending divorce.

Partners may jump to the conclusion you are tired because you have another lover or they may think you may have lost interest in them because running has turned you gay.

After training for some while, many people find all they think about is sex, and running starts to make them hot for action, resulting in them speeding up the homeward half of their training route. Alas, the mind may be sexually rampant but the body isn't and they soon find they are falling asleep during love-making which is a step forward from falling asleep before it.

Don't be concerned; as time passes you will soon begin to feel the benefit from running. Your stamina will increase and so will the sensation of physical well-being. At last you will have the hots but be in top physical condition and so be able to do something about it. Alas, this is also the time when you realise you have no partner; they have long since lost interest and gone off with someone else.

RUNNING TOGETHER

The couple who run together stay together as long as they both keep to the same schedule so their fantasies and capabilities coincide. If your partner misses a week's training, then so should you, otherwise you find your stamina is unequal to their fantasies.

Training together does have its problems. For example, running on a hot day in clothes that leave little to the imagination may give you an urge to lose yourselves in the long grass. Try to resist such temptations for the sake of your pulse rate and the laws of the land.

You will find that the experience of training together brings you closer to each other than ever before, not only sexually but mentally. You will be spending more time in each other's company and many more evenings at home. This is because you are both as boring as hell and no one wants to hang out with guys who just prattle on about running every waking moment. So make an effort to get out and about. Go to parties and meet people but try to avoid the swapping parties, the nude cocktail parties and the 'Hey, let's all throw our car keys into the centre of the room' parties. Otherwise neither of you will have the strength left for training.

Running Together

YOUR SOCIAL LIFE

The main effect running has on your social life is to make it vanish altogether. Without realising it, you can become a bore if all you want to do is talk about your P.B., jogger's nipple and stabilizers. Even old friends will start to avoid you like the plague.

They will cross you off guest lists because you are always tired in the evening with the result that you are no longer invited out to dinner. No one wants a guest who falls asleep face down in the first course, or lies with his head on the table snoring during the coffee. It somewhat diminishes your reputation as a live wire and raconteur.

Running also leads to a deterioration in your appearance, as you no longer get asked out you cease to buy new clothes. Instead, you shamble about wearing a track suit, muttering about health food and sneering at people who smoke.

More serious is the damage that can be done to your career. If you run to work or in the lunch hour no one wants to share an office with someone dripping with sweat and whose steaming feet burn holes into the carpet. Promotion will also elude you because the higher you climb in the business, the more often you are obliged to have long, large lunches and nights out with dignitaries. Falling asleep on them or scowling when they light their cigars are not attributes that will make you popular.

LISTENING TO YOUR BODY

Runners are either accused of being hypochondriacs or they are hypochondriacs. Either way their everyday conversations are punctuated by references to aches and pains or more exotic injuries.

The main problem facing a runner is how to distinguish between hypochondria, a genuine injury or a warning signal. Should you seek immediate treatment or run through the pain in the hope that somehow it will mysteriously vanish? It is possible to run through certain pains, but chest pains have to be crawled through preferably in the direction of a hospital.

Injuries can be cured by various means; physiotherapists, osteopaths, acupuncturists or faith healers can all play their part. They work on the principle that the more weird the cure, the more likely it is to work. On the whole, the idea of running is to increase the body's state of well-being and this is possible to do if you believe injuries don't get in the way of feeling well.

The only way to stop injuries is to stop running. So you must be prepared to live with them, in which case you will find them a great comfort seeing you no longer have anyone else to live with.

ALCOHOLISM

Running dehydrates the body leaving the runner with a thirst and the most natural thing to do after a run is to quench it with a drink. The ill-advised runner decides to satisfy his thirst with beer. He is amazed by the number of beers that vanish down his throat when previously he struggled over a single glass.

After downing far too many pints of beer, he wakes the following morning feeling terrible and decides to run and sweat the alcohol out of his system. But running makes him thirsty. So he resorts once more to beer. In no time at all, he becomes one of the ashen-faced, unshaven runners dripping with sweat and staggering around a local park followed by concerned off-duty nurses.

Corpse-like, the drinker pours himself from one bar to another convinced he doesn't have a drink problem, but of course he does. He can't afford to buy any more drink and so he turns to crime.

To avoid creeping alcoholism, avoid alcohol, which may mean not joining a running club. You will also find that soft drinks can satisfy your thirst without being habit forming. The simplest way to tell if you have a drink problem is to ask yourself a question and answer it with absolute honesty. 'Do you go out training with a six pack?' If you do, then you have an immediate problem. After running for several miles they explode everywhere when you open them.

BECOMING THIN

Marathon running is much talked about as being the ultimate challenge. For some people this may be true but for many others they only run to be thin, because fat is unhip. Looking thin is looking good, preferably with a suntan. Surplus mounds of white lard begin to vanish soon after taking up running, not only because exercise burns off unwanted calories but also through the worry caused by your marriage breaking up and your work prospects being wrecked.

Thinness also comes about because of a change in your eating habits. Now that you live on your own you tend to eat less because it really isn't much fun cooking for yourself. Restaurants are out too, as eating in them on your own isn't much fun and no one will eat in them with you.

Initially, you may find that running makes you hungry and so you eat more. But after a while you start to fit in eating around your training. The truth is you don't like returning to an empty home. So you stay out training for longer, which in turn means you have less time for eating.

Even those rare couples still living together change their eating habits. They no longer have the huge meals they used to because they are too busy endlessly bonking.

Becoming Thin

CHANGES IN YOUR BODY

On first seeing a group of experienced long-distance runners together you will be overawed by their collective thinness. This is achieved not only by the reasons given on the previous page, but also through the tremendous pressures confronting the modern runner. How will they pay their mortgages if they fail to finish in the first three and will they lose their sponsorship if they become injured again?

As your unwanted bulk fades away your body begins to assume a different shape. The beer gut, or post-natal pounds, fall away leaving you looking quite streamlined. You look better than you have ever done. It is almost impossible not to look at yourself admiringly every time you pass a mirror.

This is a period in your training known as 'self love'. Once you become infatuated or obsessed by your own body you don't mind running through the streets showing it off to its best advantage. Every vestige of shyness will vanish.

Unable to stop rubbing cream into your skin, stroking yourself and breathing huskily up against your reflection you will stop feeling lonely.

You have all the company you need, yourself; and what damn fine company it is.

Changes In Your Body

CHAPTER 4

THE RUNNERS

THE CHARITY RUNNER

Watching the London Marathon on television, one frequently sees a clown running backwards while tossing a pancake in the air. This apparent lunatic is not plucked from the field by men in white coats because he is running for charity. The aim, more likely than not, is to raise money for some piece of medical apparatus or a new hospital, of which he, if he does not train correctly, will be the main beneficiary. The majority of these runners indulge in the minimal amount of preparation for their runs. Their efforts appear to be focused on the fancy dress costumes they will wear to hobble in around the course. In most cases these consist of schoolgirl or nurse's uniforms for either women or men.

While watching a race, it is quite common to see grown men dressed as Vikings holding a replica longboat, waiters running with trays full of drinks, Mickey Mouse and even Superman rushing on their way. As the race progresses highly comical scenes can be witnessed: Vikings riddled with cramp and hardly able to limp let alone loot, pillage and rape; Mickey Mouse slumped on a pavement outside a bar awash with beer; or Superman running into 'the wall' and staggering in anguish as though someone had slipped some Kryptonite into his tights.

The Charity Runner

THE HERBERTS

There are two types of Herbert, and both are running's answer to a Wally or a Nerd.

Firstly, there is the Lone Herbert who has watched marathons on television. He has seen guys picking up girls en route and believes a girl of ample proportions and desires may be attracted to him. This will never happen. If he was lying on the ground needing the kiss of life there would be no takers, not even if money was on offer.

He wears shorts that were once part of his school football kit, a 'Real Ale' T-shirt with holes in it, odd socks and old tennis plimsoles caked in mud and stained by unknown substances.

Secondly, there are the group Herberts who run in packs. During marathons they wave at TV cameras, produce hand written signs that read 'Hello Mum', stop off for a pint and a fag and make such witty remarks at passing girls as 'Get them off'.

They wear cut-off denim jeans or Union Jack shorts, various parts of rugby kits and T-shirts depicting hedgehogs making love or with messages that read 'I'm on TV' or 'Hello Mum'.

They appear to be very attached to their mothers. None of their mothers have yet been sighted wearing T-shirts saying 'Hello Son'. It is understandable why.

The Herberts

THE PERSONAL BEST

Wearing a shock-proof and water-proof digital watch complete with a lap timer, a stride timer and an inhalation and exhalation timer, the PB takes to the road. A smile curls his top lip when he realises he has reached the first lamp post on his regular training route in a personal best time. Pounding along the road wearing his 'Sub Four' T-shirt, nothing is capable of breaking his concentration if he thinks a personal best time is possible. Houses may be burning, people may be screaming for help and eccentric millionaires may be giving away bundles of fifty pound notes, yet through it all the PB will not falter in his rhythm.

With his eyes permanently flickering from side to side he boils eggs, mows the lawn and reads newspapers in ceaseless competition with the clock. His manic and exaggerated behaviour has resulted in his marriage breaking down. His wife long since gave up trying to persuade him to aim at endurance records rather than speed records in the matrimonial bed. A breathless 'It was a personal best for me, how was it for you?' is a question she never wants to hear again.

The Personal Best

THE DUFFER

The Duffer is basically a walker. He may wear a running kit but he still walks. His stumbling gait is not a running action at all but he still enters every available marathon.

Hours after the race when sponsors have packed up their free chocolate bars and silver foil blankets, the Duffer staggers up to where the finishing line once was. Looking briefly about, he observes a total lack of welcoming faces for the last man home. With a blank expression he turns and walks towards the nearest station at a faster speed than he raced at.

He is a pleasant old chap and proud of the fact that he is the most ancient competitor in any of the races he enters.

Television interviewers delight at the thought of him pegging out at any moment and try to speed up the process by using up all his breath interviewing him before the race.

In certain quarters, however, he is regarded as devaluing the sport by his presence, a threat likely to open up the flood gates to nannies pushing prams, ambling window shoppers and even hitch-hikers. If this happens, the marathon will be determined by its duration, not its distance.

The Duffer

FLYING ELBOWS

Flying Elbows is the runner who overstates every movement he makes. At certain stages in a marathon when runners are pressed closely together this man can kill. His granite-like, pointed elbows are capable of piercing steel plate and when he pumps them through the air he leaves in his wake heaps of walking wounded. Eyes are knocked out of their sockets, appendixes burst, bones are shattered and wind well and truly knocked out of bodies.

His knees are equally lethal weapons. They shoot into the air as he dead-legs and gooses his way through the field. Even his eyebrows leap up and down threateningly on his forehead.

Many years ago, he thought he would develop a style to improve his times. Instead of conserving energy enabling him to run faster he acquired a style that used up energy. However, he is happy with it because it provides a sensation of greater speed.

Observing this man passing a liquid intake station is like witnessing a road accident. He sends plastic cups, sponges and helpers all flying into the air, destroying the station completely and depriving those who follow of any refreshment. Always stay in front of this man.

Flying Elbows

THE PANTOMIME HORSE

The Pantomime Horse consists of two runners inside a costume made to resemble a horse. The skills required by these runners include the ability to run for long distances with their backs bent and with only a small amount of oxygen available to them. Because of the intimate nature of sharing such a suit and the proximity of one partner's head to the other's rear, it is also necessary to be trusting friends. Although it may be considered rather extrovert to enter races dressed as a horse, both the hind and front legs are shy introverts, hence their need to appear in the most public of places without anyone knowing who they are. This shared crippling shyness can sometimes cause them great embarrassment when they are training. If it rains their costume becomes so wet and heavy that they have to leave it at home and run in normal kit, one behind the other with their backs bent and blushing to the soles of their feet. Alas, an even greater embarrassment is when one or the other is ill and training has to be done alone. Running in a public place dressed just as the front, or even worse, the hind legs, of a horse is almost as bad as running alone without the suit, bending one's back and all the time pretending not to be doing anything out of the ordinary.

The Pantomime Horse

THE MATCHSTICK

The Matchstick is in her early twenties with dark hair and a pale complexion. She is so desperately thin that she almost fails to cast a shadow. But still she runs to keep her weight down. Obsessed by maintaining her skeletal figure, she has resorted to making a lettuce leaf last for a complete week and to running at every moment available to her. She runs to and from work, in the evenings and during the lunch hour (which no longer has any meaning for her).

The matchstick is now so slight that running has actually become dangerous for her. She is constantly pulled off course when she is sucked into the slipstream of passing cyclists. She is not intent on staying paper-thin to make herself more attractive to men. On the contrary, she hates the very idea of men because of their association with calories. They are always saying to her 'Can I take you out for a meal?' or 'Fancy a drink?' without realising the grief they are causing her. Without doubt she is a truly amazing runner, gliding over the ground with delicate ease and possessing enormous stamina which contradicts every known theory concerning running. Interestingly, the more she evades men the more they are intrigued by her and pursue her as best they can; which is usually half a mile before they collapse with exhaustion.

The Matchstick

THE IRON MAN

The Iron Man is so called because of the extreme amount of pain he can take without complaining. If his legs were to be suddenly severed at the knees he would not drop out of a race. He would merely grit his teeth and complete the course still hoping to get near his personal best without making any excuses if he fails to do so.

Dressed in a sweat-soaked running kit complete with head and wrist bands, the Iron Man trains over extreme distances each week. While he is running dogs break their fangs on his calves, mothers pull their children out of his path and badly parked cars are left with dents in the shape of track shoes across their bonnets and roofs.

His unshaven face and the scars on his knees (from countless cartilage operations) give him the appearance of a badly wounded war veteran. The image is further enhanced by the manic staring eyes of a man who has been on one mission too many. Floods, Arctic conditions, nuclear strikes and the earth tilting on its axis will never stop this man from his regular training runs because the Iron Man can crack walnuts with his eyelids. He works as a cashier in the High Street Bank and answers to the name of Dorian.

The Iron Man

THE WHINGER

The Whinger is one of the most obnoxious of all runners. He is never satisfied with any meal prepared for him; the meat is red when everybody with any sense knows people should only eat white; there are either too many calories or too few; and he remains convinced that everything has been poisoned by chemicals. Similarly, he is adamant that there is a conspiracy against him buying a pair of running shoes to fit his feet.

Medically, he is a hobbling disaster. The room where he lives is lined with medical books and detailed diagrams of the body. This reference material is highly important to him. From it he can conjure a multitude of new complaints or symptoms when he has grown tired of the old ones.

The Whinger's legs and feet are permanently threatening to drop off. Enough cartilage has been removed from his knees to fill a Safeway trolley, and his ankles alone have been X-rayed more times than Princess Di has been photographed, all according to him. It is a miracle that he can breathe let alone walk. His landlady has been threatening to have him thrown out ever since he moved in. She is certain that with all the moaning and groaning coming from his room after midnight, he must have a woman in there with him.

The Whinger

LOTTY

Lotty is short for 'She who moves about a lot', in other words a woman of substantial proportions who lacks any control over her surplus fleshy parts. Where the Incredible Bulk is firm and solid, Lotty is loose and wobbly.

Running was initially a great embarrassment to Lotty and she only ventured out on the darkest of nights, developing her first traumatic strides into a semi-jog and then into a respectable trot. The daylight appearances in public no longer cause her any discomfort.

In the distance, as she approaches you, the sound of her feet slapping against the roadway can be heard followed by the disconcerting noises caused by the various parts of her body colliding rhythmically together.

Lotty has never managed to lose weight by running. But she has greatly gained in confidence as witnessed by the now forceful manner in which she thrusts her trolley through Saturday's shoppers in the supermarket.

When it comes to chocolate bars, she remains the most competent, all-devouring black hole in the universe. But she is equipped with a wonderful sense of humour which she very much needs, otherwise she may suddenly start to take seriously the food shortage she is causing in the third world.

Lotty

THE INCREDIBLE BULK

The Incredible Bulk, or Mobile Mountain as she is sometimes called, is not a wobbly fatty but a solidly rotund heavyweight for whom even the Fibre Diet failed to shift her unwanted foothills of flesh. The extra weight she carries is enormous and it places such a strain on her heart that on a still, quiet morning you can hear it moaning.

Encouraged to run in an attempt to lose weight for obvious medical reasons, she took to the public highways without a hint of embarrassment. Her neighbours soon became used to her training runs after several of them initially reported earth tremors to the police. And Doreen in number 17, for the first time in ten years of marriage, felt the ground move under the Sunday morning sheets.

Running, quite naturally, gives her an appetite which results in her eating more food which in turn leads to her weight remaining constant. However, running does provide her with a feeling of good health and well-being while also firming up her body. Her flexed stomach muscles are capable of snapping any prodding index finger.

Many other runners feel that she should be equipped with a flashing hazard light and a siren during races because, if a runner stops with his hands on his knees while gasping for breath and she suddenly crashes into him from behind, the result could be fatal.

The Incredible Bulk

THE BODIES BEAUTIFUL

The Bodies Beautiful are cohabitants on the move. They are most usually a man and woman. There may well be other sexual permutations but they all run to be seen.

Head bands, wrist bands and even ankle bands, adorn this young couple of urban professionals. They choose their designer running kits to complement each other. Equally tanned and flushed with health food they take to the road when there is the maximum amount of people to appreciate them in full flight. They are the epitome of the leisure orientated generation (i.e. those not unemployed) and as soon as their day's work is over it's on with the track suits or casual wear and off on a jog for a chilled glass of white wine in the local wine bar.

The BB's bodies are their hobbies. When they aren't looking at them in the mirror they are rubbing cream into them or having them massaged, waxed and tanned. They also exhibit them with far greater flourish and style than the Tate Gallery has ever achieved with their exhibits.

Alas, they are fair-weather runners. When the mornings and evenings cool and it is no longer comfortable to wear silk shorts split to the thigh, they no longer run. Instead, they seek out the land of the midwinter tan or spend a few weeks on the piste.

The Bodies Beautiful

THE POSEUR

The Poseur is a more extreme singular version of the Bodies Beautiful. Unlike them he is not a Yuppie. His profession is being a poseur; all his time and energy is put into looking good while running.

He runs during the various rush hours when there is the maximum amount of people to admire his style and body. He dresses in all the latest running fashions.

The Poseur is averse to speed work. Firstly, it allows people less time to observe him, and secondly, it reduces the time he stays out in the sun which will not benefit his tan. He also regards breaking into a sweat in a public place as rather uncool.

The Poseur is neither a macho man nor a medallion man. He is not trying to prove his masculinity, which may be a very dubious thing to do anyway, he is trying to prove how wonderful he looks to whoever or whatever happens to be around at the time. Women, men, children or stray dogs; as long as they form an audience, he cares not.

The Poseur never actually enters marathons anymore. He always claims to have pulled a muscle on the eve of a race. He only ever ran the London Marathon once and secretly swore never to run it again because the photograph of him crossing the line was so dreadful.

THE CLUB RUNNER

The Club Runner is a social animal. He is someone who likes to run with the pack.

After training with some of the other Club Members, he likes to slip into a local ale house with them and consume a few unriotous pints while talking about Charlie Spedding. They mostly talk about how Charlie enjoys a few pints without it stopping him from winning the odd major. Some nights they spill out into the street convinced Charlie would never have won a single major if he didn't raise the elbow regularly.

The Club Runner normally trains after finishing a day's work, covering about thirty-five miles a week. Although he is a plodder, he is a serious enthusiast and enters every available race. He will even drag himself from the sick bed should the lads need him in a competition.

Running provides him with more than an excuse to get out and have a few pints with the lads. It is also a refuge from 2.5 children and a wife. Not being a particularly fast or nimble thinker it also provides him with a space for uncluttered thoughts. In fact there are moments when he borders on being quite philosophical, usually about Charlie Spedding.

THE BODY PUNISHER

An ideal training run for the Body Punisher is up a potholed, cobblestoned hill, strewn with broken bottles and with a two-in-one gradient, leaning into a gale force wind driving sleet into his face, pulling behind him a perambulator filled with lead weights and wearing spiked track shoes inside out. To be struck by lightning or a Cruise missile would really ice his cake.

The Body Punisher longs to run into 'the wall'. He yearns to collide spectacularly with the nearest available pain barrier; only then will he reach that moment of exquisite ecstasy which he knows running to hold in store for him.

A single man, only an even greater masochist would live with him, he spends his time between runs either in a bath tub filled with ice cubes (to prepare for extremely cold running conditions), lying on top of a radiator, switched to maximum, whilst eating sand (to prepare for hot, arid conditions) or lying on the kitchen floor wearing a paper bag containing a boiling kettle over his head (to prepare for hot, humid conditions).

Running with his lips drawn back over his gritted teeth, his head at such an angle that it almost rests on his lowest shoulder and sweat pouring across his hollow, pale, unshaven face he may appear to be in great distress. Under no circumstances offer him any help or you will ruin his day. Being snapped at by a rabid dog could damage your health.

The Body Punisher

THE OBSESSIVE

The Obsessive lives for running but can't run for a living because he isn't good enough. Unfortunately, just beneath the surface of his well shaken brain, he believes that one day he will produce a time that will elevate him to world class. He fails to recognise the truth that he is not a natural runner and blames his diet, clothing and training for not being able to crack two hours twenty minutes.

His book shelves are stuffed with hard backs, paperbacks and backless backs on the subject of running. Some are written by respectable authorities on the subject and others by Californians with theories about nut diets and star signs. Stacked beside these are articles from the sports pages of newspapers and running magazines; some pages are yellowed and stained by adoring kisses or tears.

Friendless, divorced and forced to live in a cramped bed-sitting room he spends his time making notes and training. At present he is going through a phase of sitting under a pyramid to re-energise, soaking his feet in vinegar, inhaling a mixture of steamed herbs and concentrating on a fish diet. Alas, his recovery rate has deteriorated. He blames this on anxiety brought about by a neighbour's preference for playing reggae through the night disturbing his regular ten-hour sleep (with head pointed towards the magnetic pole). This man has the ability to become the new Charles Bronson. Neighbours beware!

The Obsessive

THE SHUFFLER

The extraordinary thing about the Shuffler is how he appears not to be running at all and yet completes the marathon consistently in less than three hours.

He is in his fifties, bald, wears pebbled glasses and is an engineer. His insignificant appearance makes it all the more galling when he pads silently past you within sight of the finishing line. While you are riddled with cramp, have hamstring trouble, crave a visit to a toilet or are suffering spasms, the Shuffler glides past you as though he is standing on a pedestrian conveyer belt. No matter by how much you break your personal best, he still breasts the finishing tape before you.

A clue to the Shuffler's success appears to be his leg action or lack of it which has been perfected so as to expend a minimum of energy. His legs never bend at the knee, neither do his feet ever leave the surface of the road by more than half a centimetre. In fact, wet conditions can be a danger to him. He risks losing control by aquaplaning.

If you should wish to run in a similar style to the Shuffler, do not spend money on an expensive pair of designer running shoes; carpet slippers will do just as well.

The Shuffler

THE BORN-AGAIN RUNNER

The Born-Again Runner was in his late thirties when he first
suffered ill health brought about by the pressures of work.
Realising these pressures would not improve, on doctor's
advice he decided to counter them by becoming physically
fit. He chose running as his means to stable health.
Using his gold credit card he purchased his kit from Harrods
Olympian Way and then correctly attired took to his well
manicured local avenues. In a matter of months he became a
vegetarian, acquired a tan and developed an even more
relaxed, confident manner when dealing with people.
Success in business soon followed and in no time he was
offered the role of Managing Director of the advertising
agency he had joined as a junior.
The Born-Again Runner now finds pasty food and wheezy
colleagues quite unbearable. He discourages smoking in his
presence, cools towards those who stagger back after three
hour lunches with stunned livers and he insists on having a
bowl of fresh fruit on his desk but never an ashtray.
His fitness has improved immeasurably and now he has a
great deal more stamina for his extra-marital affairs. A health
bore he may be, but prior to taking up running he was an
overpaid, self-indulgent, drunken overgrown schoolboy.
In fact, an even bigger bore.

The Born-Again Runner

THE APPARITION

The Apparition stands well over six feet and yet weighs no more than an anorexic field mouse. His long thin limbs and strangely unweathered anaemic skin give him the appearance of a starved and obscenely plucked ostrich. He is forced to wear woollen gloves throughout the year because his hands (hanging so far away from his body so that his blood fails to reach them by the process of circulation) remain continually cold.

Dressed in a running kit that resembles an escaped lunatic's underwear, flanked by outsize woollen hands and so pale-skinned his blue veins have the appearance of biro drawn running maps, the Apparition is a startling sight. His lack of visual appeal combined with his habits of humming symphonies when running, emitting sudden whoops of genteel delight at the sight of small birds and training only at twilight or dawn, can mean an encounter with him has fatal consequences.

Many an elderly gent has been out walking his pooch in the early hours and has suddenly become aware of the silently running Apparition at his shoulder overtaking him while simultaneously exclaiming a series of startling chords from Beethoven's 1894 overture. The elderly gent usually drops like a stone clutching his chest. Oblivious to the impact his life has on others, the Apparition returns home to eat a nutburger and read his truly obscure books.

He is never placed in a marathon but always finishes the course, although no one ever notices.

The Apparition

CHAPTER 5

THE RACE

THE NIGHT BEFORE THE RACE

The fashion at the moment is to attend a pasta party on the night before a marathon to load up the body with carbohydrates. The pasta is often accompanied by a little Guinness because of its mineral content. It is important not to overdo the eating and drinking in case you put on unwanted pounds or become inebriated and lust after one of your fellow competitors, wasting your training at the last moment.

Carbohydrates are energy food and are easily absorbed into the bloodstream. The last thing you want before you run is a lump of indigestible matter interned in your stomach. Neither do you want to eat gas-producing food like beans or fresh bread not only because of the discomfort you may suffer but also because of the discomfort you may cause your fellow competitors to suffer.

Be prepared to spend a sleepless night suffering from nerves; it happens to most runners especially the first time. On the other hand if you want to have a few beers and go to a discotheque, what the hell! Everyone has a different body chemistry and you may be able to get away with it. On the other hand you may completely ruin your chances in the race. The decision is yours and can be made easier by cutting a pack of cards.

The Night Before The Race

THE MORNING OF THE RACE

The big day is here. Make sure you eat something no later than three hours before the race begins and check your kit bag. You will need to take a jar of vaseline to rub into those parts of the body that may rub together or against a foreign body. Plasters must be taken in case you miss a part of your body that rubs against another part.

You will need a spare kit in case it rains and you don't want to be left dripping wet after the race. For different reasons, toilet paper is essential. When you arrive at the start everyone will be suffering from nerves and frequenting the toilets. The heavy usage of these portable havens will mean a rapid unrolling of paper. It is extremely important that you should not hold back from going to the toilet; nothing is worse than wanting to go during the race. It can cause great anxiety resulting in unwanted tension and cramp. The only alternative is to take pills which stop you going altogether, but try them out some weeks before the race so you will not worry about whether they will work or not.

You will also need a large plastic rubbish bag with head and arm holes cut into it. Last, but not least, remember a stop watch, not only to tell you the time you finished the race in, but in case you are not doing too well it will tell you when to stop and catch the last train home.

AT THE START

The first thing to strike you when arriving at the start are the crowds. You will have to fight your way through them miles away from the starting line and the nearer you get the worse they become.

The main crowd will be waiting for vacant toilets. Go if you must and then settle down to do your warming up exercises. These will be difficult to do in a confined space but they will help to initiate you into the intimate nature of a marathon race. Try to avoid lying down to perform your exercises otherwise other competitors may come and lie on top of you to do theirs, or so they will claim.

A cup of coffee at this point will help break down the fat in your blood while you are running. Avoid drinking too many cups like the fools who have to queue to use the toilets again. Next, strip down to your running kit and place your clothes in a bag which will be waiting for you when you finish. Put on the plastic bag you brought with you as though dressing in a shirt. It will keep you dry if it is raining and will contain your body heat while you are doing your final exercises. Take care; exercising in a confined space in plastic clothing can have a strange effect on one in fifty people and you will be surrounded by a lot of fifties.

At The Start

THE START

The start of the race will be signalled by people around you
roaring with delight and throwing parts of their clothing into
the air. Slowly you will move forward, so do not throw away
your plastic bag until you are at least trotting.

Almost immediately you will come across your first charity
runner. He or she will ram you from behind and turning to
swear at the culprit, you will be confronted by a maniacally
grinning gorilla, Superman or, even worse, the legendary
glue-damaged pantomime horse. Remember your training
and don't waste energy by killing anyone. Breathe deeply
and continue to move forwards as best you can.

During this initial mile you will also be hampered by the
media freaks and Herberts. These are competitors who are
prone to leap up and down a great deal. Do not worry. They
are not brain damaged or dangerous; they are trying to be
picked out by the television cameras. The whole point of the
race for them is to get onto the screen and be seen by
their mothers.

At the end of the first mile, the competitors around you will
have wilted after jumping up and down, shouting, slapping
each other on the back and wasting energy by similarly
frivolous means. This is either where your serious race begins
or the pantomime horse gets you just behind
the knee again.

The Start

THE FIRST FEW MILES

Fortunately, the first few miles are run comparatively slowly because of the volume of traffic which stops first-timers from starting off too fast.

Being wedged in a crowd of runners can be dangerous when the nearest one to you is a non-stop talker who deflects your hostile stares and proceeds to tell you about his past year's training and then goes into detail about his present injuries and ailments. Some you have heard of but begin to feel you share. Don't continue to be a listener; put in your ear plugs and hum loudly.

The almost tortoise-like pace can break your concentration making you aware of the watching crowds. The street parties, too, look inviting and so do the bars with their doors flung open and the smell of beer floating out of them. The cruellest cut of all is the lip-smacking aroma of Sunday lunch being cooked, because as everyone knows marathons are always run on Sundays.

At the point where your will-power is at its weakest, matching your knees perfectly, the race suddenly speeds up and gaps start to appear in front of you. At last you can escape the pantomime horse and if a television interviewer should obstruct your path trying to talk to you, pretend you are foreign; most runners do.

A FEW MILES MORE

Sensitive people may become offended as the race begins to take shape. The effort of running combined with the proximity of fellow competitors can lead to unpleasant aspects of the human condition. Running heightens the senses and also makes people sweat. By sniffing your fellow runners' moist bodies you can tell what they had to eat the previous evening.

Often in the first half of a race you can feel so good that you want to push on and do a better time than you initially planned. Don't make this mistake. You may feel good now but in seconds you may feel terrible. Relax into your stride and don't be put off by people who pass by sniggering at your pace. You will see them again face down in the gutter as you glide by.

It is essential to resist offers of sweets and pints of beer the crowd may so generously offer you. Don't be tempted by their invitations and, whatever you do, don't start to think 'What am I doing this for? Is it all worth it?' Above all, if someone shouts out from a window above the street, 'Hey big boy! Fancy a good time cheap?' try and believe she is shouting at someone else, and if she looks the image of your childhood sweetheart, pinch yourself and remember running can make you hallucinate . . . with any luck.

A Few Miles More

'THE WALL'

There may come a time during the race when you feel full of
energy and convinced you could finish in less than two hours
walking off with the first prize. Suddenly, this feeling of
euphoria evaporates and in a state of confused horror you
find it almost impossible to raise one foot and place it in front
of the other. Finishing the race no longer concerns you.
Covering the next metre becomes the problem.

Your body has reached the point where it is no longer
obeying messages from the brain and instead of travelling
along at a steady jog you are wobbling around in circles like a
break-dancing jelly while the race goes on around you. You
have hit the legendary 'wall' head-on and the remainder of
the race will be a living hell or worse.

The reason for you running into 'the wall' is basically
because you haven't any energy left due to incorrect training
or not guzzling enough pasta the previous evening.

With sheer will-power and determination you can still finish
the race if you're lucky by remembering to keep moving
forward. The most important thing at this stage is not to be
wearing jewellery or be carrying a wallet because you are
now an ideal target for muggers.

'The Wall'

THE COMPETITIVE SPIRIT

Once you are in the last quarter of the race and have avoided colliding with 'the wall' you are still susceptible to feeling psychologically unwell. The loneliness of the long-distance runner is well documented. It is also quite well filmed and strange things may be going on in your head. A small mysterious voice may be whispering, 'Give up, you Dork! What on earth are you trying to prove? Why don't you go home, have a hot bath, put your feet up and watch television?' The voice can be very convincing and it can make giving up seem to be the most logical thing to do. If you want to finish the race you must argue sufficiently well with yourself that you win. You will need to draw upon all your resources of competitiveness.

Being competitive means not stopping for someone who drops to the ground in front of you. After all, it is not your job to give the kiss of life to some stranger who may well be in possession of a terminal virus. Neither is it your business if someone who has smacked into 'the wall' is so confused that he staggers in the opposite direction to the race or towards a long drop into the nearby river.

Being competitive means asking yourself what you have got to lose: your marriage has broken up; the kids don't live with

114

you anymore; your bed-sitter is small and damp; and you've
just lost your job. So you might as well go for it because
'When you've got nothing, you've got nothing to lose'.

NEARLY THERE

The race is almost completed. In the distance you can see the finishing-line and the noise of the crowd has reached fever pitch. The scene around you is similar to the 'Valley of Death' after the 'Six Hundred' had charged down it. Human beings and pantomime horses are scattered over the ground. Medical staff move solemnly between the fallen raising the T-shirts of some of the victims over their faces. And vets raise pistols to the heads of the pantomime horses delivering the coup de grâce to the poor beasts as they lie on their backs, pointing their twitching legs towards horsey heaven. Suddenly, through bloodshot eyes you see a figure in the crowd wearing a black hooded cape and running a finger along the blade of the scythe he is holding. It is the Grim Reaper and he is looking right at you.

Trembling on the edge of mortality, terror floods through your wheezing veins when you hear a voice in the crowd shout out 'Number 456378! Come on 456378! You can do it, keep going, don't be a limp-wristed wimp!' Other voices take up the call and begin to chant your number. Pride engulfs you and you force yourself onwards into areas of pain where you have never ventured before until you feel as though an elephant has just sat on your chest. You are suffering a heart attack brought about by those sick sadists who always stand near the end of a race encouraging runners to permanently damage themselves.

Nearly There

THE FINISH . . .

A banner stretches across the road in front of you bearing the legend 'The Finish'. You stagger towards it with celestial music bursting your ear drums and, miracle of miracles, fireworks begin exploding in your brain as you cross the line. An official immediately grabs hold of your arm and says, 'Don't hang about please, there are other people to finish. Move along, move along. Haven't you got a home to go to?' Someone then attempts to smother you in baking foil as girls with full mouths and bodies force the sponsor's products on you. Fortunately, these are usually food and drink and not haemorrhoid suppositories.

Without knowing what is happening, you find yourself sitting all alone looking like a chicken ready for the oven, incapable of performing any post-race exercises and feeling like you could sleep for a year.

Having a few post-race beers is not a bad thing, but avoid solid food for at least three hours after the race otherwise it will pass right through you.

The most important thing at this time is to be true to your word and keep the promise you made repeatedly to yourself during the last three quarters of the race . . . never again, never again . . .

The Finish . . .

. . . AND BEYOND